50 Sweet and Savory Breakfast Recipes

By: Kelly Johnson

Table of Contents

- Classic Buttermilk Pancakes
- Scrambled Eggs with Cheese
- Blueberry Muffins
- Avocado Toast with Poached Egg
- Cinnamon French Toast
- Bacon and Egg Breakfast Burrito
- Chocolate Chip Waffles
- Spinach and Feta Omelette
- Banana Bread
- Sausage and Egg Biscuit Sandwich
- Greek Yogurt with Honey and Nuts
- Smoked Salmon Bagel
- Apple Cinnamon Oatmeal
- Breakfast Quesadilla
- Croissant with Ham and Cheese
- Peanut Butter and Banana Toast
- Veggie Breakfast Hash
- Almond Butter and Berries Toast
- Chia Seed Pudding with Mango
- Huevos Rancheros
- Strawberry Shortcake Pancakes
- Biscuits and Gravy
- Granola with Yogurt and Berries
- Savory Cheese and Herb Scones
- Sweet Potato Hash with Eggs
- Lemon Poppy Seed Muffins
- Breakfast Tacos with Chorizo
- Dutch Baby Pancake with Berries
- Egg and Cheese Croissant Sandwich
- Honey Glazed Breakfast Ham
- Maple Pecan Oatmeal
- Spinach and Mushroom Quiche
- Apple Turnovers
- Baked Avocado with Egg
- Chocolate Croissants

- Breakfast Fried Rice
- Pumpkin Spice Waffles
- Cheddar and Chive Biscuits
- Ricotta and Fig Toast
- Protein-Packed Smoothie Bowl
- Everything Bagel with Cream Cheese
- Sweet Cornbread with Honey Butter
- Shakshuka (Eggs in Spicy Tomato Sauce)
- Cherry Almond Granola Bars
- Cheesy Grits with Fried Egg
- Mocha Overnight Oats
- Ham and Swiss Breakfast Casserole
- Almond Croissant Bake
- Turkey and Egg Breakfast Wrap
- Raspberry Danish

Classic Buttermilk Pancakes

Ingredients:

- 1 cup all-purpose flour
- 1 tbsp sugar
- 1 tsp baking powder
- ½ tsp baking soda
- ¼ tsp salt
- 1 cup buttermilk
- 1 egg
- 2 tbsp melted butter
- ½ tsp vanilla extract

Instructions:

1. In a bowl, whisk together flour, sugar, baking powder, baking soda, and salt.
2. In another bowl, whisk buttermilk, egg, melted butter, and vanilla.
3. Combine wet and dry ingredients, mixing until just combined.
4. Heat a non-stick pan and pour batter to form pancakes.
5. Cook until bubbles form, then flip and cook until golden brown.
6. Serve with butter and maple syrup.

Scrambled Eggs with Cheese

Ingredients:

- 4 eggs
- ¼ cup milk
- ½ cup shredded cheddar cheese
- 1 tbsp butter
- Salt and pepper to taste

Instructions:

1. Whisk eggs, milk, salt, and pepper in a bowl.
2. Melt butter in a pan over medium heat.
3. Pour in egg mixture and cook, stirring gently.
4. When eggs are almost set, stir in cheese.
5. Cook until cheese melts and eggs are fluffy. Serve warm.

Blueberry Muffins

Ingredients:

- 1 ½ cups all-purpose flour
- ¾ cup sugar
- 2 tsp baking powder
- ½ tsp salt
- ½ cup milk
- ⅓ cup vegetable oil
- 1 egg
- 1 tsp vanilla extract
- 1 cup fresh blueberries

Instructions:

1. Preheat oven to 375°F (190°C). Line a muffin tin with liners.
2. In a bowl, mix flour, sugar, baking powder, and salt.
3. In another bowl, whisk milk, oil, egg, and vanilla.
4. Combine wet and dry ingredients, then fold in blueberries.
5. Fill muffin cups and bake for 18-20 minutes.

Avocado Toast with Poached Egg

Ingredients:

- 1 slice whole-grain bread
- ½ avocado, mashed
- 1 egg
- 1 tbsp vinegar (for poaching)
- Salt, pepper, and red pepper flakes

Instructions:

1. Toast the bread until golden brown.
2. Bring water with vinegar to a simmer and poach the egg for 3-4 minutes.
3. Spread mashed avocado on toast and season with salt and pepper.
4. Place poached egg on top and sprinkle with red pepper flakes.

Cinnamon French Toast

Ingredients:

- 4 slices bread
- 2 eggs
- ½ cup milk
- 1 tsp cinnamon
- 1 tsp vanilla extract
- 1 tbsp butter
- Maple syrup and powdered sugar for serving

Instructions:

1. In a bowl, whisk eggs, milk, cinnamon, and vanilla.
2. Dip each bread slice into the mixture, coating both sides.
3. Melt butter in a pan over medium heat and cook bread until golden brown on both sides.
4. Serve with maple syrup and powdered sugar.

Bacon and Egg Breakfast Burrito

Ingredients:

- 1 large flour tortilla
- 2 eggs, scrambled
- 2 slices bacon, cooked and crumbled
- ¼ cup shredded cheese
- 2 tbsp salsa

Instructions:

1. Warm the tortilla in a pan.
2. Place scrambled eggs, bacon, cheese, and salsa in the center.
3. Fold in the sides and roll tightly into a burrito.
4. Serve warm.

Chocolate Chip Waffles

Ingredients:

- 1 ½ cups all-purpose flour
- 2 tbsp sugar
- 1 tbsp baking powder
- ½ tsp salt
- 1 ¼ cups milk
- 2 eggs
- ¼ cup melted butter
- ½ cup chocolate chips

Instructions:

1. Preheat waffle iron.
2. In a bowl, mix flour, sugar, baking powder, and salt.
3. In another bowl, whisk milk, eggs, and melted butter.
4. Combine wet and dry ingredients, then fold in chocolate chips.
5. Cook in a waffle iron until golden brown.

Spinach and Feta Omelette

Ingredients:

- 3 eggs
- ¼ cup milk
- ½ cup fresh spinach, chopped
- ¼ cup feta cheese, crumbled
- 1 tbsp butter
- Salt and pepper

Instructions:

1. Whisk eggs, milk, salt, and pepper.
2. Heat butter in a pan and sauté spinach for 1 minute.
3. Pour in egg mixture and cook until set.
4. Sprinkle feta cheese, fold omelette, and serve.

Banana Bread

Ingredients:

- 2 ripe bananas, mashed
- 1 cup sugar
- ½ cup melted butter
- 2 eggs
- 1 ½ cups flour
- 1 tsp baking soda
- ½ tsp salt
- 1 tsp vanilla extract

Instructions:

1. Preheat oven to 350°F (175°C). Grease a loaf pan.
2. Mix mashed bananas, sugar, butter, eggs, and vanilla.
3. In another bowl, mix flour, baking soda, and salt.
4. Combine wet and dry ingredients, then pour into loaf pan.
5. Bake for 50-60 minutes.

Sausage and Egg Biscuit Sandwich

Ingredients:

- 1 biscuit (store-bought or homemade)
- 1 sausage patty
- 1 egg, fried
- 1 slice cheddar cheese

Instructions:

1. Cook sausage patty until browned.
2. Fry egg to desired doneness.
3. Slice biscuit in half and layer sausage, egg, and cheese inside.
4. Serve warm.

Greek Yogurt with Honey and Nuts

Ingredients:

- 1 cup Greek yogurt
- 2 tbsp honey
- ¼ cup mixed nuts (almonds, walnuts, pistachios)
- 1 tbsp chia seeds (optional)

Instructions:

1. Spoon Greek yogurt into a serving bowl.
2. Drizzle honey over the yogurt.
3. Sprinkle mixed nuts and chia seeds on top.
4. Serve immediately.

Smoked Salmon Bagel

Ingredients:

- 1 bagel, sliced and toasted
- 2 tbsp cream cheese
- 3 oz smoked salmon
- 2 tbsp red onion, thinly sliced
- 1 tbsp capers
- 1 tbsp fresh dill (optional)

Instructions:

1. Spread cream cheese on both halves of the toasted bagel.
2. Layer smoked salmon, red onion, and capers on top.
3. Garnish with fresh dill if desired.
4. Serve immediately.

Apple Cinnamon Oatmeal

Ingredients:

- ½ cup rolled oats
- 1 cup milk or water
- ½ apple, diced
- ½ tsp cinnamon
- 1 tbsp honey or maple syrup
- 1 tbsp chopped walnuts or almonds

Instructions:

1. In a saucepan, bring milk or water to a boil.
2. Stir in oats and reduce heat to simmer.
3. Add diced apple and cinnamon, cooking for 5 minutes.
4. Transfer to a bowl, drizzle with honey, and sprinkle nuts on top.

Breakfast Quesadilla

Ingredients:

- 1 large tortilla
- 2 eggs, scrambled
- ¼ cup shredded cheese
- 2 tbsp diced bell peppers
- 1 tbsp butter
- Salsa for serving

Instructions:

1. Heat butter in a pan over medium heat and cook scrambled eggs.
2. Place tortilla in the pan, sprinkle half of it with cheese, eggs, and bell peppers.
3. Fold tortilla in half and cook until golden brown on both sides.
4. Slice into wedges and serve with salsa.

Croissant with Ham and Cheese

Ingredients:

- 1 croissant, sliced in half
- 2 slices ham
- 2 slices Swiss or cheddar cheese
- 1 tsp Dijon mustard (optional)

Instructions:

1. Preheat oven to 350°F (175°C).
2. Spread mustard on the inside of the croissant (if using).
3. Layer ham and cheese inside.
4. Heat in the oven for 5-7 minutes until cheese melts.
5. Serve warm.

Peanut Butter and Banana Toast

Ingredients:

- 1 slice whole-grain bread
- 2 tbsp peanut butter
- ½ banana, sliced
- ½ tsp cinnamon (optional)
- 1 tsp honey (optional)

Instructions:

1. Toast the bread until golden brown.
2. Spread peanut butter evenly over the toast.
3. Arrange banana slices on top.
4. Sprinkle with cinnamon and drizzle with honey if desired.

Veggie Breakfast Hash

Ingredients:

- 1 cup diced potatoes
- ½ cup diced bell peppers
- ½ cup diced onions
- ½ cup spinach, chopped
- 1 tbsp olive oil
- 1 egg (optional)
- Salt and pepper to taste

Instructions:

1. Heat olive oil in a pan over medium heat.
2. Add potatoes and cook until golden brown.
3. Stir in bell peppers and onions, cooking until softened.
4. Add spinach and cook for another minute.
5. If using an egg, fry or scramble separately and place on top.

Almond Butter and Berries Toast

Ingredients:

- 1 slice whole-grain bread
- 2 tbsp almond butter
- ¼ cup mixed berries (strawberries, blueberries, raspberries)
- 1 tsp honey

Instructions:

1. Toast the bread until golden brown.
2. Spread almond butter over the toast.
3. Top with mixed berries and drizzle with honey.

Chia Seed Pudding with Mango

Ingredients:

- ¼ cup chia seeds
- 1 cup milk (or almond milk)
- 1 tbsp honey or maple syrup
- ½ tsp vanilla extract
- ½ cup diced mango

Instructions:

1. In a bowl, mix chia seeds, milk, honey, and vanilla extract.
2. Stir well and refrigerate overnight (or at least 4 hours).
3. Stir again and top with diced mango before serving.

Huevos Rancheros

Ingredients:

- 2 eggs
- 2 small corn tortillas
- ½ cup refried beans
- ¼ cup salsa
- ¼ avocado, sliced
- 1 tbsp fresh cilantro
- 1 tbsp olive oil

Instructions:

1. Heat olive oil in a pan and fry the eggs to desired doneness.
2. Warm tortillas in a separate pan.
3. Spread refried beans on each tortilla and top with fried eggs.
4. Spoon salsa over the eggs and garnish with avocado and cilantro.

Strawberry Shortcake Pancakes

Ingredients:

- 1 cup all-purpose flour
- 1 tbsp sugar
- 1 tsp baking powder
- ½ tsp baking soda
- ¼ tsp salt
- ¾ cup buttermilk
- 1 egg
- 2 tbsp melted butter
- ½ cup fresh strawberries, chopped
- Whipped cream and extra strawberries for topping

Instructions:

1. In a bowl, whisk together flour, sugar, baking powder, baking soda, and salt.
2. In another bowl, mix buttermilk, egg, and melted butter.
3. Combine wet and dry ingredients, stirring until just mixed. Fold in chopped strawberries.
4. Cook pancakes on a greased skillet over medium heat until golden brown.
5. Serve topped with whipped cream and extra strawberries.

Biscuits and Gravy

Ingredients:

- 2 cups all-purpose flour
- 1 tbsp baking powder
- ½ tsp salt
- ½ cup butter, cold and cubed
- ¾ cup milk
- ½ lb breakfast sausage
- 2 tbsp butter
- 2 tbsp all-purpose flour
- 2 cups milk
- Salt and pepper to taste

Instructions:

1. Preheat oven to 425°F (220°C). Mix flour, baking powder, and salt in a bowl.
2. Cut in butter until crumbly, then stir in milk to form dough. Roll and cut into biscuits.
3. Bake for 12-15 minutes until golden brown.
4. In a pan, cook sausage until browned. Remove and set aside.
5. Melt butter in the same pan, whisk in flour, then gradually add milk. Stir until thickened.
6. Return sausage to the pan and season with salt and pepper. Serve over biscuits.

Granola with Yogurt and Berries

Ingredients:

- 1 cup Greek yogurt
- ½ cup granola
- ½ cup mixed berries (strawberries, blueberries, raspberries)
- 1 tbsp honey

Instructions:

1. Spoon Greek yogurt into a serving bowl.
2. Top with granola and mixed berries.
3. Drizzle with honey and serve immediately.

Savory Cheese and Herb Scones

Ingredients:

- 2 cups all-purpose flour
- 1 tbsp baking powder
- ½ tsp salt
- ½ cup butter, cold and cubed
- 1 cup shredded cheddar cheese
- 1 tbsp fresh chives, chopped
- ¾ cup milk

Instructions:

1. Preheat oven to 400°F (200°C).
2. Mix flour, baking powder, and salt in a bowl. Cut in butter until crumbly.
3. Stir in cheese and chives, then add milk to form a dough.
4. Roll out and cut into scones.
5. Bake for 12-15 minutes until golden brown.

Sweet Potato Hash with Eggs

Ingredients:

- 1 large sweet potato, diced
- ½ onion, chopped
- ½ red bell pepper, diced
- 2 tbsp olive oil
- 2 eggs
- Salt and pepper to taste

Instructions:

1. Heat olive oil in a pan over medium heat. Add sweet potatoes and cook for 5 minutes.
2. Add onion and bell pepper, cooking until tender.
3. Make two wells in the hash and crack in the eggs. Cover and cook until eggs are set.
4. Season with salt and pepper before serving.

Lemon Poppy Seed Muffins

Ingredients:

- 1 ½ cups all-purpose flour
- ¾ cup sugar
- 1 tsp baking powder
- ½ tsp baking soda
- ¼ tsp salt
- ½ cup butter, melted
- ½ cup buttermilk
- 2 tbsp lemon juice
- Zest of 1 lemon
- 1 tbsp poppy seeds
- 1 egg

Instructions:

1. Preheat oven to 375°F (190°C).
2. Mix flour, sugar, baking powder, baking soda, and salt.
3. In another bowl, whisk together melted butter, buttermilk, lemon juice, lemon zest, and egg.
4. Combine wet and dry ingredients, then stir in poppy seeds.
5. Pour batter into muffin tins and bake for 18-20 minutes.

Breakfast Tacos with Chorizo

Ingredients:

- 2 small tortillas
- ½ cup cooked chorizo
- 2 eggs, scrambled
- ¼ cup shredded cheese
- 2 tbsp salsa
- ¼ avocado, sliced

Instructions:

1. Warm tortillas in a dry skillet.
2. Fill each with scrambled eggs, cooked chorizo, and cheese.
3. Top with salsa and avocado slices. Serve immediately.

Dutch Baby Pancake with Berries

Ingredients:

- ½ cup all-purpose flour
- ½ cup milk
- 2 eggs
- 1 tbsp sugar
- ½ tsp vanilla extract
- 2 tbsp butter
- ½ cup mixed berries
- Powdered sugar for topping

Instructions:

1. Preheat oven to 425°F (220°C).
2. Blend flour, milk, eggs, sugar, and vanilla extract until smooth.
3. Melt butter in a cast-iron skillet in the oven.
4. Pour batter into the skillet and bake for 15-18 minutes.
5. Top with berries and powdered sugar before serving.

Egg and Cheese Croissant Sandwich

Ingredients:

- 1 croissant, sliced
- 1 egg, scrambled
- 1 slice cheddar cheese
- 1 slice ham (optional)

Instructions:

1. Warm croissant in the oven at 350°F (175°C).
2. Cook scrambled eggs and place on the croissant.
3. Add cheese (and ham if using), then close the croissant.
4. Serve warm.

Honey Glazed Breakfast Ham

Ingredients:

- ½ lb ham steak
- 2 tbsp honey
- 1 tbsp Dijon mustard
- 1 tbsp butter

Instructions:

1. In a pan, melt butter over medium heat.
2. Whisk together honey and mustard, then brush over ham.
3. Cook ham for 3-4 minutes per side until caramelized.
4. Serve warm with eggs or toast.

Maple Pecan Oatmeal

Ingredients:

- 1 cup rolled oats
- 2 cups milk or water
- 2 tbsp maple syrup
- ¼ tsp cinnamon
- ¼ cup chopped pecans
- 1 tsp vanilla extract
- Pinch of salt

Instructions:

1. In a saucepan, bring milk or water to a boil.
2. Stir in the oats, reduce heat, and simmer for about 5 minutes, stirring occasionally.
3. Add maple syrup, cinnamon, vanilla extract, and salt. Stir to combine.
4. Remove from heat and top with chopped pecans. Serve warm.

Spinach and Mushroom Quiche

Ingredients:

- 1 pre-made pie crust
- 1 cup fresh spinach, chopped
- 1 cup mushrooms, sliced
- ½ cup shredded cheese (cheddar or gruyère)
- 4 eggs
- 1 cup heavy cream or milk
- ½ tsp salt
- ¼ tsp black pepper

Instructions:

1. Preheat oven to 375°F (190°C).
2. Place pie crust in a pie dish and prick the bottom with a fork. Bake for 10 minutes, then remove.
3. In a pan, sauté mushrooms and spinach until softened.
4. Whisk eggs, cream, salt, and pepper in a bowl. Stir in the cooked vegetables and cheese.
5. Pour mixture into the pie crust and bake for 30-35 minutes until set.
6. Let cool for 5 minutes before slicing. Serve warm.

Apple Turnovers

Ingredients:

- 1 sheet puff pastry, thawed
- 2 apples, peeled and diced
- 2 tbsp sugar
- ½ tsp cinnamon
- 1 tbsp lemon juice
- 1 tbsp cornstarch
- 1 egg (for egg wash)

Instructions:

1. Preheat oven to 375°F (190°C).
2. In a bowl, mix apples, sugar, cinnamon, lemon juice, and cornstarch.
3. Roll out the puff pastry and cut it into squares. Place apple filling in the center of each.
4. Fold the pastry over into a triangle and press edges with a fork to seal.
5. Brush with beaten egg and bake for 20-25 minutes until golden brown.

Baked Avocado with Egg

Ingredients:

- 1 ripe avocado
- 2 small eggs
- Salt and pepper to taste
- ¼ tsp red pepper flakes (optional)
- Chopped parsley for garnish

Instructions:

1. Preheat oven to 375°F (190°C).
2. Cut avocado in half and remove the pit.
3. Scoop out a small amount of flesh to make room for the egg.
4. Crack an egg into each avocado half.
5. Bake for 12-15 minutes until eggs are set.
6. Season with salt, pepper, and red pepper flakes. Garnish with parsley.

Chocolate Croissants

Ingredients:

- 1 sheet puff pastry, thawed
- ¼ cup chocolate chips or chocolate bar pieces
- 1 egg (for egg wash)

Instructions:

1. Preheat oven to 375°F (190°C).
2. Roll out puff pastry and cut into triangles.
3. Place chocolate on the wider end and roll into a crescent shape.
4. Brush with beaten egg and bake for 15-18 minutes until golden brown.

Breakfast Fried Rice

Ingredients:

- 1 cup cooked rice (day-old works best)
- 2 eggs, scrambled
- ½ cup cooked bacon or sausage, crumbled
- ½ cup chopped vegetables (bell pepper, onion, or spinach)
- 1 tbsp soy sauce
- 1 tsp sesame oil

Instructions:

1. Heat sesame oil in a pan and sauté vegetables until softened.
2. Add rice and soy sauce, stirring well.
3. Push rice to one side and scramble the eggs. Mix everything together.
4. Stir in bacon or sausage and cook for another minute.

Pumpkin Spice Waffles

Ingredients:

- 1 cup flour
- 1 tsp baking powder
- ½ tsp cinnamon
- ½ tsp pumpkin spice
- ½ cup pumpkin puree
- 1 egg
- ½ cup milk
- 2 tbsp melted butter
- 2 tbsp maple syrup

Instructions:

1. Preheat waffle iron and grease with butter.
2. In a bowl, mix dry ingredients. In another bowl, whisk wet ingredients.
3. Combine both mixtures and stir until smooth.
4. Pour batter into the waffle iron and cook until golden brown.

Cheddar and Chive Biscuits

Ingredients:

- 2 cups flour
- 1 tbsp baking powder
- ½ tsp salt
- ½ cup cold butter, cubed
- 1 cup shredded cheddar cheese
- ¼ cup chopped chives
- ¾ cup milk

Instructions:

1. Preheat oven to 400°F (200°C).
2. In a bowl, mix flour, baking powder, and salt.
3. Cut in butter until the mixture resembles coarse crumbs.
4. Stir in cheese and chives, then add milk. Mix until just combined.
5. Drop spoonfuls onto a baking sheet and bake for 12-15 minutes.

Ricotta and Fig Toast

Ingredients:

- 2 slices of bread
- ¼ cup ricotta cheese
- 2 fresh figs, sliced
- 1 tsp honey
- 1 tbsp chopped nuts (optional)

Instructions:

1. Toast the bread until golden brown.
2. Spread ricotta cheese on top.
3. Arrange fig slices and drizzle with honey.
4. Sprinkle with nuts for extra crunch.

Protein-Packed Smoothie Bowl

Ingredients:

- 1 banana
- ½ cup Greek yogurt
- ½ cup almond milk
- 1 tbsp peanut butter
- 1 scoop protein powder (optional)
- ½ cup mixed berries
- Granola for topping

Instructions:

1. Blend banana, yogurt, milk, peanut butter, and protein powder until smooth.
2. Pour into a bowl and top with berries and granola.

Everything Bagel with Cream Cheese

Ingredients:

- 1 everything bagel, sliced and toasted
- 2 tbsp cream cheese
- Optional toppings: smoked salmon, capers, sliced tomato, red onion

Instructions:

1. Toast the bagel to your desired crispness.
2. Spread cream cheese evenly on both halves.
3. Add any optional toppings as desired.

Sweet Cornbread with Honey Butter

Ingredients:

- 1 cup cornmeal
- 1 cup flour
- 1/4 cup sugar
- 1 tbsp baking powder
- 1/2 tsp salt
- 1 cup buttermilk
- 2 eggs
- 1/2 cup melted butter

For the Honey Butter:

- 1/2 cup butter, softened
- 2 tbsp honey

Instructions:

1. Preheat oven to 375°F (190°C). Grease a baking pan.
2. In a bowl, mix dry ingredients. In another bowl, whisk wet ingredients.
3. Combine both mixtures and stir until smooth.
4. Pour batter into the pan and bake for 20-25 minutes.
5. For honey butter, mix butter and honey. Spread over warm cornbread.

Shakshuka (Eggs in Spicy Tomato Sauce)

Ingredients:

- 1 tbsp olive oil
- 1/2 onion, diced
- 1 red bell pepper, diced
- 2 cloves garlic, minced
- 1 tsp cumin
- 1/2 tsp paprika
- 1 can (14 oz) crushed tomatoes
- 4 eggs
- Salt and pepper to taste
- Fresh cilantro for garnish

Instructions:

1. Heat oil in a skillet over medium heat. Sauté onion and bell pepper until soft.
2. Add garlic, cumin, and paprika, cooking for 1 minute.
3. Pour in crushed tomatoes, season with salt and pepper, and simmer for 10 minutes.
4. Make small wells in the sauce and crack in the eggs. Cover and cook until eggs are set (about 5 minutes).
5. Garnish with cilantro and serve with bread.

Cherry Almond Granola Bars

Ingredients:

- 2 cups rolled oats
- 1/2 cup almonds, chopped
- 1/2 cup dried cherries
- 1/4 cup honey
- 1/4 cup almond butter
- 1/2 tsp vanilla extract
- 1/4 tsp salt

Instructions:

1. Preheat oven to 350°F (175°C). Line a baking dish with parchment paper.
2. In a bowl, mix oats, almonds, and dried cherries.
3. Heat honey, almond butter, vanilla, and salt in a saucepan until smooth.
4. Pour over dry ingredients and mix well.
5. Press mixture into the baking dish and bake for 15 minutes. Let cool before cutting into bars.

Cheesy Grits with Fried Egg

Ingredients:

- 1 cup grits
- 3 cups water or milk
- 1/2 tsp salt
- 1 cup shredded cheddar cheese
- 1 tbsp butter
- 2 fried eggs

Instructions:

1. Bring water to a boil, then add grits and salt. Reduce heat and cook for 10-15 minutes, stirring occasionally.
2. Stir in butter and cheese until melted.
3. Top with fried eggs and serve warm.

Mocha Overnight Oats

Ingredients:

- 1/2 cup rolled oats
- 1/2 cup milk
- 1 tbsp cocoa powder
- 1/2 tsp instant coffee
- 1 tbsp maple syrup
- 1/4 cup Greek yogurt

Instructions:

1. Mix all ingredients in a jar or bowl.
2. Cover and refrigerate overnight.
3. Stir before serving and top with chocolate chips or nuts if desired.

Ham and Swiss Breakfast Casserole

Ingredients:

- 6 slices bread, cubed
- 1 1/2 cups diced ham
- 1 cup shredded Swiss cheese
- 6 eggs
- 2 cups milk
- 1/2 tsp salt
- 1/4 tsp black pepper

Instructions:

1. Preheat oven to 375°F (190°C). Grease a baking dish.
2. Spread bread cubes evenly in the dish. Add ham and cheese on top.
3. Whisk eggs, milk, salt, and pepper, then pour over the bread mixture.
4. Bake for 35-40 minutes until golden and set.

Almond Croissant Bake

Ingredients:

- 4 croissants, torn into pieces
- 1/2 cup sliced almonds
- 2 eggs
- 1/2 cup milk
- 1/4 cup sugar
- 1/2 tsp almond extract

Instructions:

1. Preheat oven to 350°F (175°C). Grease a baking dish.
2. Place croissant pieces in the dish and sprinkle almonds over them.
3. In a bowl, whisk eggs, milk, sugar, and almond extract. Pour over croissants.
4. Bake for 20-25 minutes until golden brown.

Turkey and Egg Breakfast Wrap

Ingredients:

- 1 whole wheat tortilla
- 2 scrambled eggs
- 1/4 cup diced turkey
- 1/4 cup shredded cheese
- 1 tbsp salsa

Instructions:

1. Warm the tortilla in a skillet.
2. Add scrambled eggs, turkey, cheese, and salsa.
3. Roll tightly and serve warm.

Raspberry Danish

Ingredients:

- 1 sheet puff pastry, thawed
- 1/2 cup raspberry jam
- 4 oz cream cheese, softened
- 2 tbsp sugar
- 1 egg (for egg wash)

Instructions:

1. Preheat oven to 375°F (190°C).
2. Cut puff pastry into rectangles.
3. Mix cream cheese and sugar, then spread on each pastry piece.
4. Add a spoonful of raspberry jam on top.
5. Fold edges slightly, brush with egg wash, and bake for 15-18 minutes.

www.ingramcontent.com/pod-product-compliance
Lightning Source LLC
LaVergne TN
LVHW081505060526
838201LV00056BA/2935